MW01635407

For Craig, who isn't funny - BD

Scholastic Australia
345 Pacific Highway Lindfield NSW 2070
An imprint of Scholastic Australia Pty Limited
PO Box 579 Gosford NSW 2250
ABN 11 000 614 577
www.scholastic.com.au

Part of the Scholastic Group
Sydney • Auckland • New York • Toronto • London • Mexico City • New Delhi • Hong Kong • Buenos Aires • Puerto Rico

Published by Scholastic Australia in 2014.

A Cataloguing-in-Publication entry is available for this title from the National Library of Australia.

ISBN: 9781743622469 (hbk.)

Typeset in Futura.

Printed by Tien Wah Press, Malaysia.

Scholastic Australia's policy, in association with Tien Wah Press, is to use papers that are renewable and made efficiently from wood grown in sustainable forests, so as to minimise its environmental footprint.

10 9 8 7 6 5 4 3 2 1 14 15 16 17 18 / 1

GET THE GIGGLES!

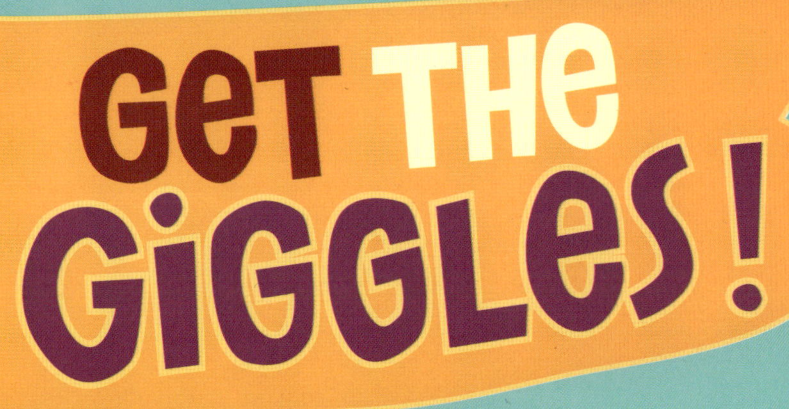

By Bronwen Davies

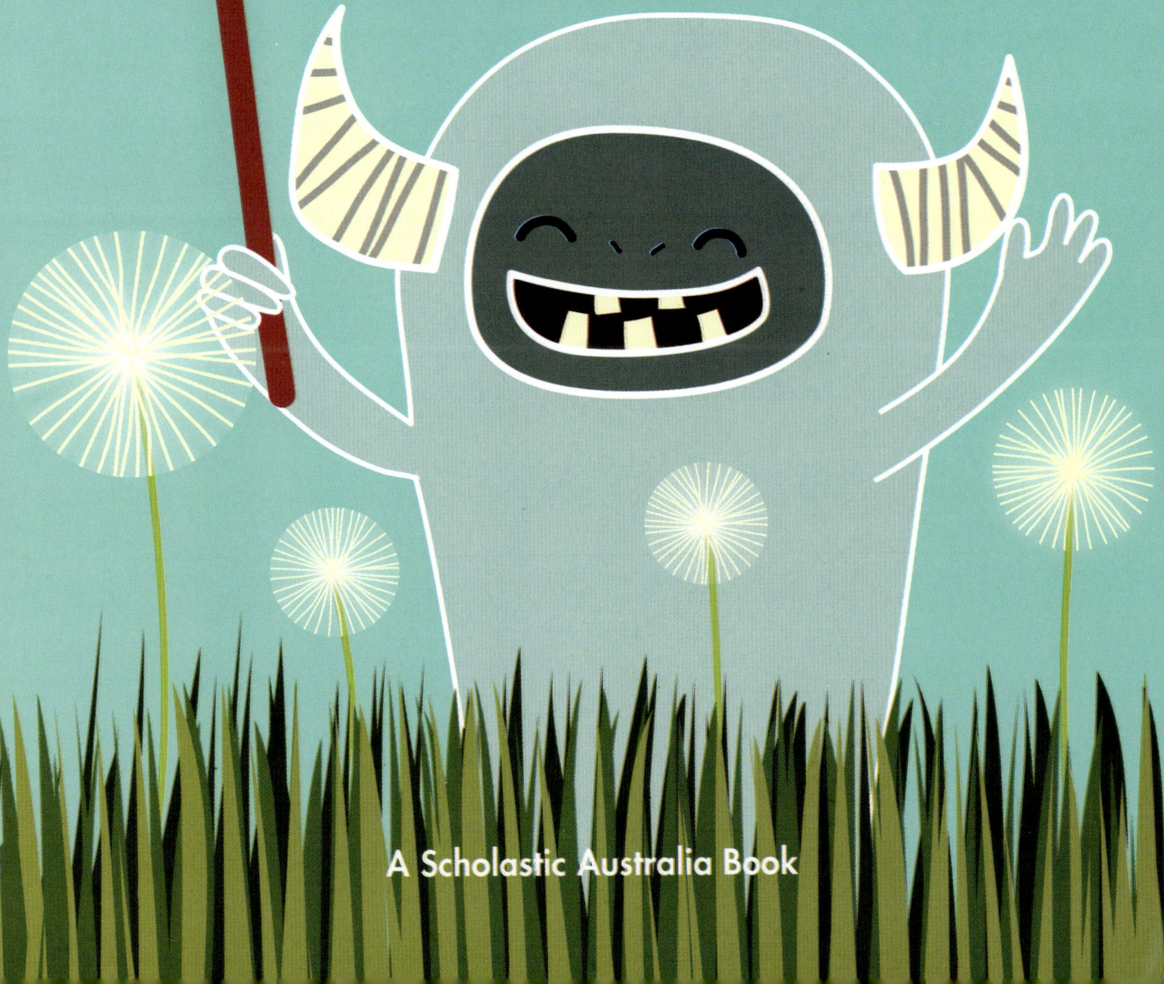

A Scholastic Australia Book

What do you call an alligator wearing a vest?

An investigator.

What do you call a fly with no wings?

A walk.

What did the fisherman say to the magician?

'Pick a cod, any cod!'

What did the dolphin say to its friend when it swam into a boat?

'You did that on porpoise.'

What do you call two banana skins on the ground?

A pair of slippers!

What do elephants have that no other animals have?

Baby elephants.

What do you call a polar bear wearing earmuffs?

Anything you want—it can't hear you!

What did the doctor say when the invisible man tried to make an appointment?

'I can't see him now.'

Why did the chicken cross the playground?

To get to the other slide.

Why did the burglar take a bath?

He wanted to make a clean getaway.

What's the best way to find your dog
if you lose it in the forest?

Put your ear up to a tree and listen for the bark.

What did the cat say after it fell out of the tree?

'Meowch!'

How did the yeti get down the hill?

He rode his icicle.

Why are leopards so bad at hiding?

Because they are always spotted.

Why do only fairies sit under toadstools?

Because there isn't mushroom.

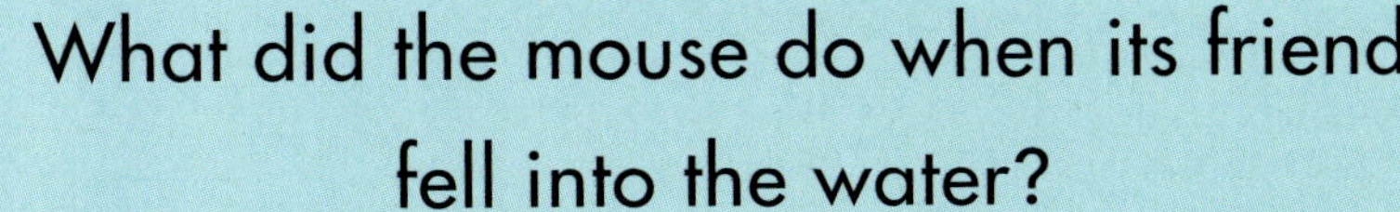

What did the mouse do when its friend fell into the water?

It performed mouse-to-mouse resuscitation.

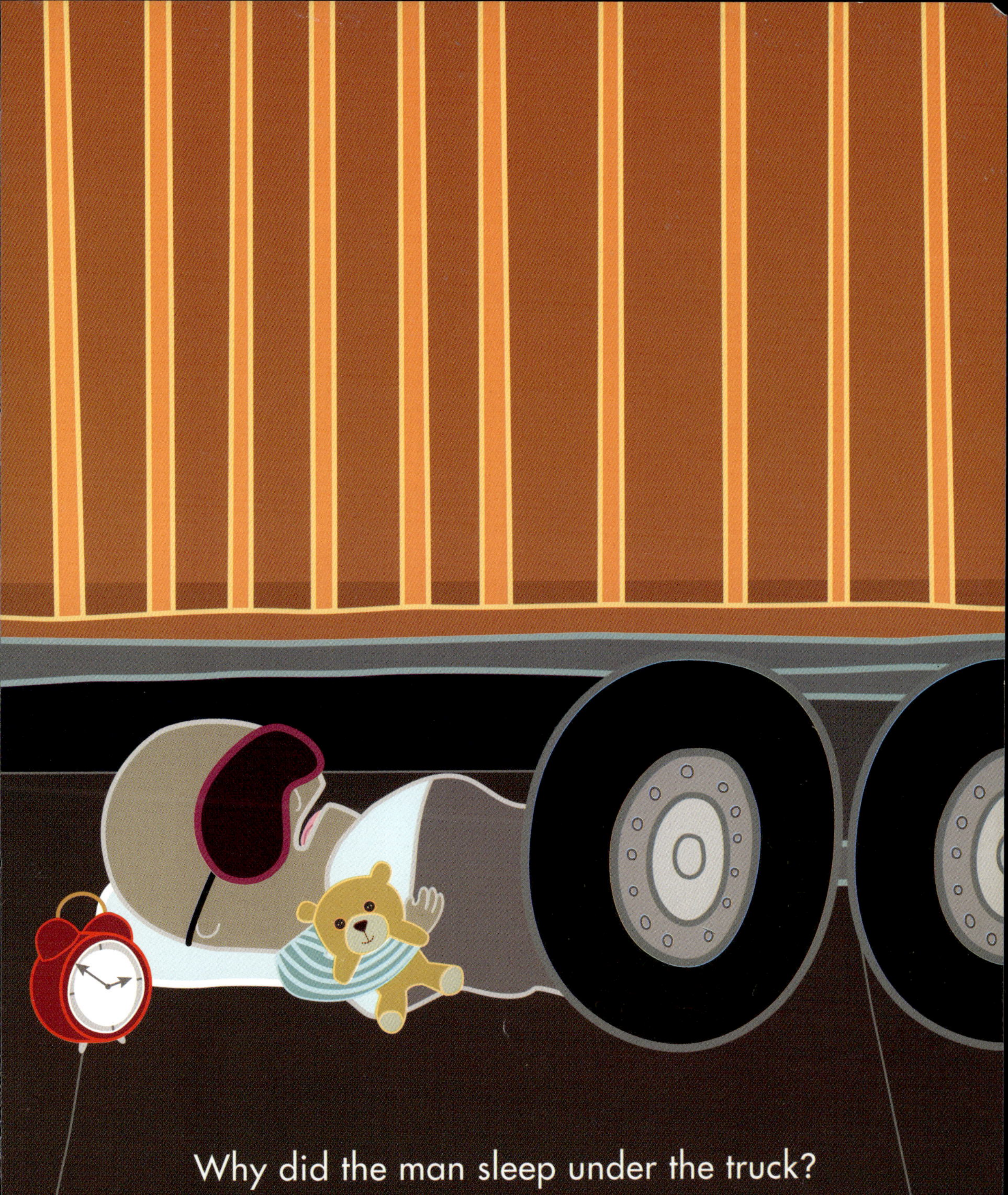

Why did the man sleep under the truck?

He wanted to wake up oily.

Why did the scarecrow win an award?

For being outstanding in its field.

What did the judge say after a skunk walked into the room?

'Odour in the court!'

Where do sheep go to get a haircut?

The baa-baa shop.

What's worse than finding a worm in your apple?

Finding half a worm in your apple!

Why do birds fly north in winter?

Because it's too far to walk.

What's the best way to catch a fish?

Have someone throw it to you.